THE LIFE AND WISDOM OF
FRANCIS
OF ASSISI

THE 'SAINTS ALIVE' SERIES

THE LIFE AND WISDOM OF

FRANCIS

OF ASSISI

Written and Compiled by

LAVINIA BYRNE

ALBA·HOUSE   NEW·YORK

SOCIETY OF ST. PAUL, 2187 VICTORY BLVD., STATEN ISLAND, NEW YORK 10314

British Library Cataloguing in Publication Data:
A record for this book is available from the British Library.

ISBN 08189 08653

Typeset in Monotype Columbus by
Strathmore Publishing Services, London N7.

Printed and bound in Great Britain by
Mackays of Chatham PLC, Chatham, Kent.

Hodder and Stoughton Ltd,
A division of Hodder Headline PLC,
338 Euston Road, London NW1 3BH

CONTENTS

INTRODUCTION

———————◆———————

Who are the saints and why should we bother to know about their lives? We are inclined to think of them as heroic people who did extraordinary things, or as people who suffered a great deal and were somehow specially gifted or good. What we then forget is that, in general, saints are people like us. They struggled to know themselves better, to be more kind and loving, more self-accepting, less neurotic. They did not always succeed. They thought their attempts to live with integrity would make them closer to other people and to God. Often what they then discovered was that other people became harder to love and that God simply disappeared.

Yet they kept up the struggle. They believed that they were given one chance, that they had to live with a certain generosity, because this life is a preparation for the full glory of the next life. They then learnt that we are given many chances because all is grace, and the Christian life is a life of grace. So their schemes and plans for being holy were dismantled. All that was asked of them was a readiness to accept the gifts of God, including the final gift of heaven.

Saints come from every walk of life. They are men and women who share our concerns about money, power, politics, peace, energy, food, war, death, sex, love, privacy, the inner life, the outer life, harmony, balance. What makes them distinctive is that they looked beyond themselves to know how best to live and they discovered that God shared their concerns. If we read about them nowadays, we do so out of more than simple curiosity. Their lives are worth reading because we can learn from them. We look for more than a good example, though. The saints seem to know more than we do; they have access to a deeper level of wisdom than our own. They are gurus for our times. So when we read about them, we are quite right to seek an insight into the mind of God, who calls and inspires us all to the heroism of holiness, however we ourselves happen to live. Holiness is for all, not just the few; for a holy life is no more than a life lived in the presence of God.

In our materialistic and agnostic age, do the saints still matter? Have they any wisdom for us, or are they simply a pious irrelevance? A thirteenth-century merchant's son may not seem like an obvious spiritual leader, yet his influence is still experienced in our own times. For Francis of Assisi is one of the most popular and famous of the saints. His concerns are concerns we all share. He knew and understood about the importance of the material world. He knew about nature, or what we call the environment; he knew that things matter and that we are inclined to define ourselves in terms of the things we possess or own. Furthermore, we are sometimes tempted to think that we are what we own, and that we own the people we love. Francis throws light on our anxieties. He asks the bigger questions about what we value and why.

In Part One of this book, we discover the story of his early life. Part Two shows how he came to maturity. It offers an interpretation of Francis and his importance for nowadays. He was more than a nature saint, more than a poor man who did good. Francis was a naked man, a man who dared to stand as he was in the presence of God. Part Three gives an insight into the mind of Francis with prayers and texts from his own writings.

There are legendary stories about Francis which make him out to be a deeply simple and uncomplicated man, a friend of the animals and a troubadour for his own ideals of poverty. The truth is much more interesting and much more important for us, as Francis is a saint with wisdom for our times.

PART ONE

The Story of His Early Years

The seal of the kingdom of heaven

PART ONE

The seal of the kingdom of heaven

The moment of truth

Francis took off all his clothes and stood naked before his father and the bishop. With that radical gesture, Western Christendom was transformed. A rich young man handed himself over to total love and service of the gospel. Ultimately he became a saint.

We know him as Francis of Assisi, for he is named after his native city, Assisi in Umbria in central Italy. In his own times, he travelled well beyond its confines: physically, emotionally and spiritually. He went on pilgrimage to Rome, to Jerusalem and followed the footsteps of the Crusaders by travelling to Acre. He journeyed emotionally because he fell in love with an idea and it turned his life around: the 'Lady Poverty' became his ideal. He grew spiritually as well, because he found that the literal rebuilding of the Church which first attracted him to the love and service of God in fact had a much bigger meaning than he first realised. He is one of the best loved of all the saints, attracting people from every church – and from none – by the sheer enthusiasm and simplicity which drove him. Here was a man in whom the love of God became visible: his love of God and God's for him.

In every age Francis has had followers, people who have turned to his life for inspiration. He has been held up as an example of fidelity, of the absolute value of the call to follow Christ. Recently he has been seen as an early advocate of 'green' issues, an early environmentalist whose affection for animals put him into a special and harmonious relationship with God's creation. He has become an apostle of simplicity and an apostle of love.

How are we to find inspiration in the life of this merchant's son as we face the millennium and the demands of a new age? How does Francis configure for us today? Quite unusually among the saints, he grappled with things that are still important to us nowadays. The body, money, possessions, debt — all of these were the fabric of his journey to God. In the western world they remain of genuine concern to us now. We are aware of our need to look at them and think about them as creatively as possible. His were middle-class concerns, the concerns of the rising bourgeoisie. Only a merchant's son, with a background in barter and trade and material reality could make a spiritual pilgrimage which would incorporate these things into the fabric of the Church's imagination as Francis did. He understood that possessions and our attitude towards them are terribly important. His was a new asceticism for a new age. The medieval period was coming to an end; the Renaissance had yet to begin. Francis stood at a crossroads. That is why he has wisdom for us now as we too face a crossroads in our own times.

So we need to listen to his story again for it has wisdom for us too. Its high point is that moment of stripping, when he first embraced the 'queen of virtues', the Lady Poverty. This is a filmic moment. It could be captured on television and would look as sensational to us as it was then. Was Francis crazy or what, at that moment of truth when he took off all his clothes and stood naked in front of the two most important authority figures in his world? One was his father, the other was his bishop.

What brought Francis to this moment? Why was the rich merchant, Pietro Bernardone of Assisi, so enraged by his son? And what about his mother, Pica? What did she make of this strange behaviour? Here was the elegant young man who had done so well and brought so much credit to his family, stripping off in front of them and unceremoniously giving back every shred of clothing into his father's hands. The bishop hastened to have a cloak put round him and then found him a simple tunic. But the power of the moment stayed with him. It would inform the rest of his life. So was it anything more than an act of rebellion against his father? Or was it something important for the Church as well as for Francis? For our own times, as well as for thirteenth-century Italy?

PART ONE

How the story begins

The story begins in 1182. Francis was born while his father was abroad on a trade mission to France. Hence his name. His mother had him baptised Giovanni, calling him after John, the beloved disciple of Jesus who stood at the foot of the cross, a name that already called him to a special relationship with the Lord. When his father returned, flush with orders for the fabrics he sold, he renamed him Francisco after his time in France. It is thought that his mother Pica was in any case French, a native of Picardy. So Francis was named after a successful business trip. Yet all the time, in the background, his other name spoke volumes: it called him to love.

His father continued to prosper and to heap the benefits of his wealth on to Francis, who enjoyed a good education, fine clothes, smart friends and, in his late teens, the opportunity to go to war. A skirmish between Assisi and Perugia gave him the chance, but also led to his imprisonment, as his side lost. In prison, his companions complained about him. His relentless good humour got them down. Eventually, though, he fell ill and on his release, he returned to Assisi. But now he found that he had lost some of his enthusiasm for the social whirl. Nevertheless, he still thought he was meant to be a professional soldier and bought a suit of armour. He was to be a knight, to become more noble and upwardly mobile than his parents. The world was his oyster. But already something had been de-stabilised in Francis and the experience of prison had opened his eyes to another way of living, a much simpler, more ordinary way of being.

He was supposed to leave Assisi for a war with Apulia, a chance to win his spurs and to make a great name for himself. But as he prepared to leave, he met another soldier of noble birth who was stricken by poverty and whose clothes were unequal to his calling. Francis felt sorry for him and gave him his own armour. The journey into stripping had begun. The seal of the kingdom of heaven was upon him. For he was about to learn that poverty is more than an affliction, a disaster which strikes out of the blue. It can also be a calling and can bring great blessings and freedom.

That night he dreamt of a weapons store, full of military equipment. When he asked who it belonged to, he was astonished to find that all these arms were his. He began to realise that he had resources at his disposal. He was a rich young man. So the following day, when he set off for the war, he was confident that he had what it took. Another dream that night, at Spoleto, shook him to the core. 'Where are you going?' a voice asked. 'To Apulia, to become a knight,' he replied. And so it was that he heard the words: 'Which is it better to serve, the master or the servant?' The answer was a simple one: 'The master, of course.' 'Then why do you serve the servant instead of the master, the poor instead of the rich?' his dream persisted. Then he knew that God was speaking to him. He said, 'Lord, what do you want me to do?' The answer was direct: 'Go home, there you will be told what to do.'

Dreams of war and the fruits of war in the form of a knighthood were over, a whole new journey was about to begin. So Francis returned to Assisi to wait upon God's will. He gave a banquet on his return, but seemed moody and preoccupied. 'Have you fallen in love?' his friends asked expectantly. 'Yes,' he replied, 'I have, and she is nobler, richer and lovelier than any other.' Francis, like many a romantic young man, had fallen in love and, in the tradition of the times, he used the language of courtly love to describe his feelings. For the woman in question was the Lady Poverty, and with her emergence into his consciousness, his great journey had begun.

What is it about poverty which both attracts and repels? Was it easier for Francis because his was a pre-industrial world where poverty might mean simplicity but not grime and squalor? When a call to poverty is a call to simplicity, it sounds deeply attractive. Where it is a call to misery, it should be resisted at any cost because it implies an exploitative relationship where some succeed at the expense of others and casualties are created on a horrific scale. Francis in fact pushed both these definitions to a new place: he understood that the call to poverty is a call to embrace one's own God-given humanity.

Pilgrimage to Rome: the first of his journeys

After the banquet with his friends, Francis set off to Rome to visit the tomb of St Peter. In the symbolic ordering of things, this flight to the very centre of the Catholic Church is a significant one. If his family and his little town were no longer to be his centre, then he would need a new one. But he had to make a real journey within time for it to be stamped on his self-understanding. Francis needed things to be real, and sealed on him. That is why he was led to the point when he would strip off his own clothes. He did things which made perfect sense to him, because he understood that it was important to act out what was happening inside himself. That is also why, eventually, at the end of his long journey, just before he died, he would be stamped with the seal of the stigmata. The crucifixion of Jesus would be marked on his very flesh.

For the moment, though, the journey to Rome was something of an adventure, and not a particularly pleasant one. For a refined young man, the choices he made were extreme. He went to St Peter's, emptied his purse, exchanged clothes with a beggar and sat at the church door, begging for alms in French – a new language as he struggled with a new identity.

When the time came for his return to Assisi, he again heard words from heaven: 'Francis, you must now learn to despise and hate what you have hitherto loved in the flesh, if you understand my will. And once you have begun to do this, you will find that all that was bitter and hard becomes sweet and pleasant, and all that you thought of with gloom and terror will bring you happiness and peace.' The promise was one of freedom.

This is why the life and spiritual heritage of Francis are so important. His was not the choice of a simple lifestyle for its own sake, nor an early ecological vision where harmony with nature would be assured by his own actions. Now this is an insight which we badly need at the moment, because much contemporary interest in nature sentimentalises it. For Francis, nature was not a friendly environment or even an environment to be befriended. It was where he chose to live and what gave him his food. He might be baffled by some of the concerns voiced by present city dwellers about the state of the countryside, or by the desire we have to save time and take shortcuts in our production of food. He had no choice but to go with the rhythms of light and dark and the seasons. He lived within nature, within created reality.

He certainly did not act out of guilt: the son of a rich man did not suddenly develop a social conscience about the poor and needy around him. Rather he tested and made choices within the set of experiences with which he was most familiar – money, clothes, trade, exchange. And then he chose poverty because it promised him happiness. It restored his humanity to him, rather than diminishing it.

The leper's kiss

Now, as Francis returned home from Rome, a further trial awaited him. He knew he had found the object of his heart's desire in the Lady Poverty, and talked about her nobility, her richness and her loveliness, because he had fallen in love with her and she had become more real a figure to him than those on the pages of the literature of courtly romance. He had tested his love for her by experiencing something akin to the condition of the homeless, squatting on the ground and begging. But now he needed a mirror image of himself, someone utterly poor and despised whom he could embrace and who could reflect back to him the true cost of his choices. How could he be shown that he was to accept his own humanity with total simplicity and humility, and that he could do so without shame? This was the man who had ridden away to be a knight. A glittering, golden youth, a man with a deeply simple, generous, loving heart.

That is when God put a leper in his path. As he was riding along, Francis saw this grossly deformed man. He gave a gift to the leper and kissed his hand. The leper seized the initiative. He pulled Francis towards him and kissed him on the lips. 'Set me as a seal upon your heart, as a seal upon your arm; for love is strong as death, passion fierce as the grave' (Song of Songs 8.6).

'Go, rebuild my Church'

Francis needed concrete things and concrete experiences. His spiritual journey was anything but abstract. It was marked by tangible landmarks, and the next one was the little Church of San Damiano. This was a tumble-down building near Assisi where Francis would go to pray. One day, when he was kneeling before the crucifix there, he heard the naked figure of Jesus say to him: 'Francis, do you not see that my house is falling down? Go and rebuild it.' 'Yes Lord, I will,' he answered. And being a fairly literal man, he went outside, gave money to the priest for the purchase of oil and a lamp to burn before the crucifix and took off home to find some funds for the restoration of the building.

Once home he spotted a bale of some particularly fine material, loaded it on his horse, set off for nearby Foligno and sold the horse and the cloth on the market place there, in front of the church of Santa Maria infra Portes. Later he would write a prayer to Mary, the Mother of Jesus, to whom this church was dedicated. It is an astonishing piece of writing, for the images come tumbling out. Buildings, clothing, temples, houses career into each other as he struggles to put his feelings into words. This is the prayer of a cloth-merchant's son.

Hail Mary, blessed Lady, queen most holy, mother of God, perpetual virgin. From the heights of heaven, you were chosen by the most holy Father, consecrated by him and by his most holy dear Son and by the Spirit, who is the Comforter. The fullness of grace and the wholeness of grace dwell in you.

Hail, for you are the palace of God!

Hail, for you are the temple of God!

Hail, for you are the house of the Lord!

Hail, for you are the clothing of the Lord!

Hail, for you are the handmaid of the Lord!

Hail, for you are the the mother of God!

Hail all the holy virtues through which you fill the heart of the faithful by the grace and light of the Holy Spirit.

You make disciples out of faithless people.

Francis the disciple took the money from his sale straight to the priest at San Damiano who was, of course, terrified, being only too conscious of the authority of Pietro Bernardone. He refused to take the cash and Francis tossed it on to a window-sill and went away into the woods to begin a life of prayer and searching in a local cave. When he felt ready to leave the cave, he set off for Assisi and the confrontation with his frantic, angry father. He was haggard and looked a wreck. People could barely recognise him. Yet on he went to his parents' home and submitted to their anger. It was Guido, the Lord Bishop of Assisi, who finally arbitrated between Francis — who described himself as a servant of Christ alone — and his parents, whose sense of shock and outrage are hard to imagine.

A new life for Francis
It was at this moment that Francis stripped off all his clothes and his new life began. Once more, he set a seal upon the experience. When the bishop gave him an old tunic, so as to cover him up, he took a brick and chalked a cross in white

dust on the back of his garment before setting off on the next stage of his adventures. The year was 1206.

Gubbio was his first destination. Later the people there would tell how Francis calmed a wolf who persecuted them. 'Brother Wolf,' Francis said, 'You have been making a lot of trouble round here. You have been mercilessly attacking God's creatures, and even God's own image in human beings, and everyone is quite rightly complaining about you. But I want you to be at peace with the town, and I promise you that as long as you live the people of the town will feed you every day, but only provided you promise never again to do harm to man or beast.' The wolf put its paw in Francis' hand and shook on the agreement.

Francis too was taking up a friendly wolf's existence, one in which he would be totally dependent on the good will of townspeople to feed and care for him. At first he collected stones to rebuild his precious church at San Damiano. Then he collected for St Peter's church outside the city and finally for Santa Maria Maggiore and Santa Maria degli Angeli, also known as the Porziuncola.

On the feast of St Matthias, 24 February 1209, Francis heard more words. They came to him from Matthew's gospel this time. Having made the church his centre, he could now hear the message in a new way. The text was from chapter 10: 'Take no gold, or silver, or copper in your belts, no bag for your journey, or two tunics, or sandals, or a staff' (Matthew 10.10). The call was one to evangelical simplicity. For the man who had stripped himself of his clothes, there was further stripping to be done in the name of the gospel. He offered himself generously for it.

The beginnings of a new way of life for the Church
And, surprisingly, it was at that very moment that he himself was offered something more precious than any clothing or possession. For very soon three companions came forward and said they wanted to share his way of life. Bernard da Quintavalle was a merchant, Pietro da Cattaneo was a cathedral canon, and the third was Edigio

or Giles of Assisi. Here were friends and companions for the journey. His way of life was no longer his own; it had now become inspirational, a way for other people to find God. From now on, his own way to God would be lived within a dense network of relationships. Some of Francis' most passionate writing uses the language of relationship and of love. He wrote because he loved God; he wrote as he did because other people so loved him. It was not by chance that the sun and wind and fire would become his brothers with the moon and water as his sisters. It is not by chance that he is so conscious of the Trinitarian nature of the Godhead, where all is gift and all is relationship.

So what would their common way of life be, and what would be its spiritual underpinning? Later Francis wrote this prayer:

Almighty, eternal, just and merciful God,
grant us grace to do for you what we know to
be your will,
for we are miserable sinners.
May we desire what pleases you.

May your inward fire make us pure,
your inward light give us light,
may we be set on fire by the Holy Trinity.
May we follow in the steps of your Son,
our Lord Jesus Christ,
and come to you through your grace alone.
O most high God,
you live in perfect trinity and absolute unity
and reign in glory,
God almighty, from everlasting to everlasting.
Amen.

Francis and his brethren were miserable sinners. These words do not come easily to our lips because we are not happy with the judgment they imply. And because we fear judgment, we also fear the truth which is that we are indeed sinners and that we stand in need of redemption. None of us has been embraced by a leper, as tangible evidence of our fallen nature. Rarely have we gazed at the full wretchedness of our own condition or experienced the full strength of our need for God. We have mechanisms for denying the true extent of the harm we do when we hurt other people. Yet when we embrace our own humanity by acknowledging our sinfulness, when we experience the fact that simplicity and suffering are normal, because we are fallen beings, we are able to abandon the myth of our own perfection, the shiny armour of personal nobility and knighthood. That is when we learn that Francis was telling the truth. We come to God through the grace of forgiveness which God offers us, rather than through the merits of our own actions. All are judged at the foot of the cross and all are redeemed there.

The wider circle

So, as the life of Francis unfolds, how can it inspire us to become his followers and truly make that insight our own, just as he aspired to become a follower of Jesus, having prayed so earnestly at the foot of the cross in the little church of San Damiano? How can we become part of the charmed circle of those who are inspired by the story of Francis? Brothers flocked to the Order he founded and which Pope Innocent III ratified in 1210. Sisters too would present themselves under the leadership of Clare. A Third Order would emerge, with lay members who gave themselves to God in the way of Francis. There were luminaries among them such as Dante, Elizabeth of Hungary and, more recently, Galvani, Volta and Ampère – early pioneers of electricity – and a host of others. People of clarity and vision who turned to Francis to inspire their sense of simplicity, confident that he would help them too to strip away all that lay between them and the following of Christ.

That is what it is all about. Francis' prayer to God the Father puts this insight at the heart of his spiritual message:

> May your inward fire purify us,
> your inward light enlighten us,
> may we be set on fire by the Holy Trinity.
> May we follow in the steps of your Son,
> our Lord Jesus Christ,
> and may we come to you through your grace
> alone.

What was the heart of this inward purification?

How could the work of the fire of the Trinity be done? Francis' own answer to this question is quite clear. It comes in a prayer in praise of poverty and the intense transformation which it promises. Once he understood what a true call to poverty meant, he could write about the inspiration which led him to see that poverty is not frightening. Instead, it promises freedom and a new way of relating to God: a naked encounter with the living God, the blessed and holy Trinity.

O Lord Jesus, show me the way of your very dear poverty. I know that the Old Testament was the figure of the New Testament. You made this promise to the Jews, 'I will deliver to you every place that the sole of your foot shall tread upon' (Joshua 1.3). To tread underfoot means to scorn. For poverty puts everything underfoot and so she is the queen of everything. But, my sweet Lord Jesus Christ, have pity on me and on Lady Poverty, for I suffer because of my love for her and I can have no peace apart from her.

O my Lord, you well know that you have made me fall in love with her and now she is full of sadness, and everyone ignores her. She is like a widow who is the queen of nations. She, who is the queen of all virtues, is vile and despised. She sits on a dunghill where she weeps and all her friends despise her. They behave as adulterers and not as faithful partners. Behold, Lord Jesus, poverty is the queen of virtues and for her sake you left your throne among the angels when you came to earth. In your eternal love you married her in order to have – by her and of her – perfect sons and daughters. She was so faithfully devoted to you that she began to serve you from your mother's womb by giving you the smallest of living bodies.

When you were born from the womb of a Virgin, poverty welcomed you in the holy manger, in a stable. During your stay in the world, poverty deprived you of all things, so that you had nowhere to lay your head. As a companion for life, poverty followed you faithfully when you began the battle for our salvation. In the middle of your passion, poverty alone stood beside you like a squire. Your disciples forsook you and denied you but poverty faithfully stayed with you and supplied you with the whole company of her sisters. Even your mother, who alone remained faithfully attached to you and shared your passion with so much anguish, could not reach you on your high cross. But Lady Poverty, with all her privations, was like a gentle maiden when she held you more chastely than ever as she was so intimately united with you in your crucifixion. As usual, she did not try to polish or adorn the cross. Will anyone ever believe that she did not even provide enough nails for your crucifixion? The nails were neither polished nor sharp. She only prepared three nails and they were rough, big and blunt so that you suffered even more. While you were dying of thirst, this faithful spouse saw to it that you should even be denied a little water. She also made the faithless soldiers offer you a drink that was too bitter for you to taste, let alone drink. You gave up your soul held in the arms of this spouse.

But, because she is faithful, she did not leave you at the place where you were buried.

She only allowed you to borrow the sepulchre, the spices and the linen. This holy spouse did not leave you at your resurrection either. She rejoiced in your kisses when you rose in glory from the tomb as you left behind what had been given or lent to you. Then you took her with you into the heavens as you left to the world all that belongs to the world. To Lady Poverty you have given the seal of the kingdom of heaven which is used to mark out those people who wish to walk in the way of perfection.

Oh, who then would not love Lady Poverty above everything else? I implore you to be marked with her seal. My desire is to be made rich by such a treasure. I swear to you, most poor Jesus, that on account of the love of your name I have no personal possessions. As long as I am alive in this miserable body I will always use the gifts other people give me sparingly. So be it.

Poverty does not demean us; it brings us into harmony with the choices of God and traces a seamless path from the manger to the cross of

25

Jesus. 'To Lady Poverty you have given the seal of the kingdom of heaven which is used to mark out those people who wish to walk in the way of perfection'. This is a deeply practical mysticism, and one which speaks eloquently to our times. For it asks us to examine what it means to say that the Son of God became like us, and then to ask how we may become like him. How are we to follow Jesus? Francis helps us answer that question and to explore its meaning for our own lives.

PART TWO

———————

The Wisdom of Francis

The impression of the wounds of Christ

———◆———

The impression of the wounds of Christ

The naked man reclothed

After the stripping would come the reclothing. But only those who risk the violence of this act of self-stripping can truly be reclothed by Christ. Religious faith claims to offer an interpretation of the apparent craziness of Francis' behaviour. It seeks out the true meaning of what he lived through and the choices he made. The Church has canonised him because of it, not despite it. But that does not mean that we should not ask questions about what motivated him and gave him such a strong sense of purpose. The reason for doing this is a very simple one. If God met Francis as he really was, we may take heart and also the risk of meeting God as we really are. Otherwise we dismiss him as a crank; his relationship with his father as dysfunctional; his relationship with nature as naive; his poverty as anti-materialistic; his stigmata as psychosomatic; his theology as non-existent; and his spirituality as a myth. A man who got canonised by mistake, rather than a saint.

God works with the material; God works with us as we truly are. God's dealings with the cloth merchant's son are far too important for us to write them off in the name of questionable pathology or to cover them up in the name of a mistaken piety. They require a far more careful interpretation, because we are not simply talking about Francis, we are also thinking about ourselves and our own relationship with God. We are not helped by a naive theory of our own pathology, or of what motivates us. It does us no good at all to be over-pious.

In the case of Francis, the facts are plain. The young man who set off to get away from Assisi and his father's trade by becoming a soldier – a knight even – was in fact called to engage in a brand new way with cloth and clothing, with fabric and pattern and shape, with marks and seals and design. His eye would be tested, his ability to see would be tried. Francis' spiritual domain was the material world, a sensate world, the world we in fact inhabit, a world of choices and temptations, from which he did not escape, but rather with which he engaged. That is why his real concern was with harmony, especially in our relationships with God, each other and with nature. That is also why Francis can speak to us and to our concerns. He can help us understand ourselves and our world.

The early years as a disciple of Christ

At first he and his companions lived amicably in the woods at Rivotorto, near Assisi. They had little huts to live and pray in. They visited lepers and worked in the fields for local farmers, gathering olives and wood. Here they began to develop their way of life together and they began to work out what it means to follow in the footsteps of Jesus. This has to be more than a pious desire, more than the inherent longing of the human heart for a way to the Lord. 'Make me to know your ways, O Lord; teach me your paths. Lead me in your truth, and teach me, for you are the God of my salvation; for you I wait all day long' (Psalm 25.4–5). Francis turned to prayer, penance and the Scriptures for inspiration. How was he to imitate Jesus? How were he and his first companions to live? These are questions which still preoccupy us. How can the gospel speak to us in our own circumstances? How are we to live?

The New Testament offered him several different models of discipleship. Francis wanted to 'follow in the teaching and footsteps of our Lord Jesus Christ' and 'to observe the holy gospel of God'. What is this 'imitation of Christ'? What did Francis discover about 'walking in the footsteps of our Lord Jesus Christ'? In the New Testament, the disciple is called with the words, 'Follow me,' and sets out, like Francis, faithfully imitating what Jesus does, literally following him step by step. 'Follow me' are favourite words for Matthew, Luke and, above all, for Mark, who favour the verb and never the noun *kelouthos* or path, the static concept from which we get our word acolyte. By external imitation or following, the disciple learns to participate in what is offered by fidelity to the Lord.

The gospel offered Francis one story in particular which must have seemed tailor-made for him. Mark tells us that the first of the rich young men attracted to Jesus had assured him of his own perfectibility. Francis already knew that holiness lay with God and with the new commandment to love. 'The young man said to him, "Teacher, I have kept all these [commandments] since my youth." Jesus, looking at him, loved him and said, "You lack one thing; go, sell what you own, and give the money to the poor, and you will have treasure in heaven; then come, follow me"' (Mark 10.20–21). At the heart of the gospel call to freedom is a call to identify with what God did when Jesus became man: a call to embrace humanity and to abandon one's own will to take up and live by the will of God. The way to do this, especially if you are rich, is to accept poverty.

Francis had given all he owned and followed Jesus. He had parted with his clothes, his money, his power, his influence. Now, surrounded by brethren, he sought inspiration from Jesus' other commandment: 'He called the crowd with his disciples, and said to them, "If any want to become my followers, let them deny themselves and take up their cross and follow me. For those who want to save their life will lose it, and those who lose their life for my sake, and for the sake of the gospel, will save it" ' (Mark 8.34–5). There is no point in 'poverty' for its own sake. What matters is self-gift.

This was a word for Francis and his first companions. It was also a word for Clare, the first of the women to be drawn to the way of life he pioneered. As Clare and her sisters took up residence at San Damiano in 1212, he would have to consider another text from Mark's gospel: 'There were also women looking on from a distance; among them were Mary Magdalene, and Mary the mother of James the younger and of Joses, and Salome. These used to follow him and provided for him when he was in Galilee; and there were many other women who had come up with him to Jerusalem' (Mark 15.40–41). For Francis developed a way of life which could be followed by women as well as by men, a way of life which could attract anyone and which could be embraced by anyone.

In Mark's gospel all of these words are addressed to the person who wants to re-direct his or her life in the service of the gospel. Francis knew about this literal following of Christ, the external imitation where the acolyte fits his steps into the footsteps of the Master. He knew about its attraction, but did he realise its dangers too? Did he know that it can lead to what the Reformation would call a 'doctrine of works', the desire to work out one's own salvation by sheer effort and a mechanistic literalism? Luther would say, '*non imitatio fecit filios sed filatio fecit imitatores*' – 'it is not imitation which makes us sons and daughters of God, but the divine image within which enables us to imitate.' Fitting one's footsteps in to the footsteps of Jesus is not enough. It can lead to a fundamentalism which does nothing to touch the soul, however bright one's intentions. A true following of Jesus means something even deeper and even more attractive.

This hints at another call, and this time it is addressed by John's gospel. For John understands imitation to be an interior attitude. True disciples have been taught personally by the Lord and absorb this teaching into their inner being. So, in John's gospel, Jesus says, 'Those who eat my flesh and drink my blood abide in me, and I in them' (John 6.56), and 'I am the vine, you are the branches. Those who abide in me and I in them bear much fruit, because apart from me you can do nothing' (John 15.5), and 'As the Father has loved me, so I have loved you; abide in my love' (John 15.9).

Francis knew the exultation of this mystical union. He came increasingly to abide in God. Union with God speaks to our deepest desires. It calls us to self-gift from a truly centred sense of who we are and where we are going. And Francis craved that. But he did so in an innocent, uncerebral way, driven as he was by the knowledge that Jesus had divested himself of his heavenly clothes to enter into our humanity. There is a simplicity and a directness here which make mystical union a deeply attractive choice. But, once again, he knew of its dangers too, and notably the danger of what we would call quietism, a totally passivity which sits ill beside the vocation of the brothers. After all, they were to work as well as to pray; to seek out the needy and speak to them of the love of God and to show this love in acts of friendship and plain, ordinary human kindness.

So where does balance lie? Paul writes about the *mimetai*, disciples who know that they are forgiven by God and who owe their entire being to God and to this forgiveness. This is where true freedom lies, for it hands power and control back to God. It restores the creature to a life of harmony with the Creator. It undoes the disobedience of our first parents and their fall from grace. So Francis writes, 'Let us hold to the words, life, teaching and holy gospel of Christ.' Christ the risen Lord of the Christian life gives us more than a pattern or set of rules for our imitation, more than a set of attitudes which alter the way we think and turn our deepest hearts to God. Our Lord Jesus Christ brings the transformation of grace which Francis knew in his own experience.

That is his gift to the Church. So how did the

Church at that time receive such a generous gift? How does it do so now? There is a simple but very important issue at stake here: how can you legislate for a life of grace? Can such a profound spiritual insight as that of Francis be shared with others as their 'foundational' or fundamental way of life? How can you organise a group of people who are drawn together by a vision of poverty and simplicity? Can you 'make' people have an experience like that of kissing the leper? Can you 'force' them to do the equivalent of stripping off in front of the bishop and their own father, or is that impossible? These are difficult questions. They trouble us as individuals; for we know that any generous self-offering to God has to come from the personal heart of an individual and that the true initiative lies with God. They trouble the Christian community as a whole; for, as a teaching and a praying Church, we are responsible for training others in the life of faith. How do we provide religious formation which respects God's call? How does grace work?

In search of a 'Rule'

As brothers joined him and his early companions, Francis had no choice but to write a Rule or 'way of life' for them. He would also need the Church's endorsement for it, so he had to go to Rome and seek approbation for his new Order. And this he duly did. Yet Pope Innocent III was appalled by the strictness of the Rule which Francis proposed. To his mind it was unliveable – and so it would prove to be, by all but Francis, that is.

For Francis understood that by experiencing radical poverty in obedience to the radical self-stripping of God in the incarnation of Jesus, and by practising that radical poverty, great freedom would come: the re-clothing of the human person. And these new clothes would come from God, just as the true identity of Jesus came from God. His model was the Jesus of the gospels. His was a love affair – with all the irrational feelings that come to people who are in love – and so of course self-gift came easily to him. He wanted to be where God was, as a lover wants to be where the beloved is.

A spirituality of dependency

This is the key to understanding Francis' relationship with nature. With God he found beauty in the natural world because it spoke to him of utter dependence on divine providence. 'Look at the birds of the air; they neither sow nor reap nor gather into barns, and yet your heavenly Father feeds them. Are you not of more value than they? And can any of you by worrying add a single hour to your span of life? And why do you worry about clothing? Consider the lilies of the field, how they grow; they neither toil nor spin, yet I tell you, even Solomon in all his glory was not clothed like one of these' (Matthew 6.26–9). For this reason, when we deny ourselves, what we are denying or going against is our own anxiety. Those who truly depend on God enjoy poverty and enjoy simplicity. By it they discover that they need God. So Francis could write in his 'Letter to the Faithful': 'We must follow the precepts and counsels of our Lord Jesus Christ. We must deny ourselves, placing our body under the yoke of holy obedience and servitude, according to our vows promised to God.'

To discover God, we need the freedom to observe the pattern of Jesus' love, where the self-gift of God brings Jesus to the simplicity of the manger, to the poverty of the cross, and only then to the new clothing of the resurrection. This implies a huge shift in power, away from self, towards God.

The maturing of an ideal

It took the revelation of a serious dream to change Pope Innocent III's mind about granting permission for the early Rule to be adopted by Francis. The night after their meeting and his rejection of the proposed text, as he slept, the Pope saw the Lateran Basilica falling down and Francis, the little man from Assisi, holding it up. The following day he approved the Rule. Sadly, we have no record of this document, though we know that it was used to prepare the next Rule of the Franciscans, which is dated 1221.

We return from Rome with Francis as he sets off for Rivotorto. He moved to Santa Maria degli Angeli, or the Porziuncola as it is more commonly known. Here Francis and his followers grew in the knowledge and love of God. A gradual maturing began to take place. This is a pattern familiar from the pages of the gospel. 'When they had finished everything required by the law of the Lord, they returned to Galilee, to their own town of Nazareth. The child grew and became strong, filled with wisdom; and the favour of God was upon him' (Luke 2.39–40). When the requirements of the Law are met, a deeper maturity becomes possible, where further freedom will be the norm because the favour of God rests upon those who are faithful to the divine will.

New horizons

The Order flourished and grew strong. By 1219 there were 5,000 brothers. That year, with thirteen companions, Francis visited the Crusaders and travelled with them on a ship from Ancona to Cyprus and then on to Acre and to Egypt. He was deeply disappointed by what he found. An army confronted the Moors; dialogue looked impossible. Yet he demanded access to the Sultan and visited Melek el Kamil at Danietta.

He was received most graciously and then returned via Jerusalem to Italy. This is an extra-ordinary story. It reminds us that Francis was totally a man of his age. He was concerned about the issues which drove the Church of his day, and the Crusades are the most powerful symbol of them.

Christianity became focused and centred when it developed an identifiable enemy: the Moor. It did outrageous things to the Moor – as it had done to its earlier enemy, the Jew – and it claimed that the gospel sanctioned such behaviour. Francis ran with the spirit of the age when he did something very definite to grapple with this question. He conducted his own personal crusade with all the fervour and valour of the crusading knights, but with more spiritual acumen than them. Like them, he claimed to act in God's name, riding out to engage with the foe. The brave simplicity of the soldier remained an important ingredient of his spirituality, even when he abandoned the knightly call. But there was more to it than that. He pushed back the boundaries and did not allow the Moor to be an unquestioned or an unexamined enemy. He wanted a conversation with the Sultan, and he got it.

The final stripping

In 1220, Francis resigned as the Franciscans' leader. The final stripping began, for it gradually became clear that the only way they could develop as an order would be to accommodate his ideas but to back down from the true rigour of his vision. They began to institutionalise the way of life; they built houses and undertook worthy causes. In the fullness of time they would become rich and have splendid buildings to live in and powerful advocates for their works. In the name of poverty, they would develop a watertight economy where no-one appeared to own anything, yet the institution would be rich and powerful. Francis' ideas made sense, and other people could live by them; his ideals were possibly too personal to do more than inspire a pale imitation. He continued to pray and to live as simply as he could. He continued to exhort and inspire, but exercised the lowest office he could find. He was never ordained priest, but remained a deacon to the end of his days.

It was at this time that the animal stories, which would form the basis of the anecdotes related in the *Little Flowers of St Francis,* began to proliferate – Francis with the bear or the lamb, the pheasant or the doves. These are all very well, but they cloak and sentimentalise the true journey on which he was engaged. Perhaps it was unliveable: at once deeply attractive, which is why the brothers and sisters flocked to him – and we still do – but ultimately a lone journey, a heroic journey, a journey of such utter transformation that it was more inspirational than do-able and could only ever be undertaken by a lone individual, rather than corporately by a group.

The sense of what Francis saw, and the moderation which true simplicity would bring, is captured in this exhortation:

> Where love and wisdom reign, there is neither
> fear nor ignorance.
> Where patience and humility reign, there is
> neither anger nor disturbance.

Where poverty and joy are found, there is
neither love of money nor avarice.

There is neither anxiety nor excess, where peace
and mediation reign.

Where the fear of God guards the heart, the
enemy can find no way in.

Where mercy and temperance live, there is
neither too much nor too little of anything.

— *Admonitions no. 27.*

Those words are so attractive. Characteristically
they speak to the religious aspirations of anyone,
and of everyone. They invite us to harmony and
self-understanding, whether as groups or as individuals. More would come with the true mystical
writing of Francis, where his own material reality
and the reality of creation become one, because
he has seen that creation too, like the mysteries
of the birth, life and death of Jesus, is seamless.
This is where his true understanding of natural
reality becomes a theology, and offers a vision of
great clarity and sanity.

Theology lived in nature and in grace

His greatest canticle is the Canticle of the Sun, a
paean of praise to creation and to the Creator
God:

> Most high, most great and good Lord, every
> praise, glory and blessing belong to you; they
> belong to you alone, most high God. No one is
> worthy to call you by your name.
>
> You are blessed, my Lord, for the gift of all
> your creatures, and especially for our brother,
> master sun, by whom the day is filled with
> light. He is radiant and bright, of great splen-
> dour, bearing witness to you, O my God.
>
> You are blessed, my Lord, for our sister the
> moon and the stars; you formed them in the
> heavens, and made them fair and clear.
>
> You are blessed, my Lord, for my brother
> the wind, for the air, for cloud and calm; for
> every kind of weather, for through them you
> hold all creatures in being.
>
> You are blessed, my Lord, for our sister
> water, for she is very useful, humble, chaste and
> precious.

You are blessed, my Lord, for brother fire, bright, noble and beautiful, untameable and strong, by whom you make light in the night.

You are blessed, my Lord, for our mother the earth, who sustains us and gives us food, producing all kinds of fruit, herbs and brightly coloured flowers.

You are blessed, my Lord, for those who forgive each other because they love you, and patiently bear infirmity and tribulation.

Happy are those who abide in peace, most high God, for you will crown them.

You are blessed, my Lord, for our sister death of body, from whom no living person can escape. Woe to those who die in mortal sin. Happy are those who at the hour of death are found to be obedient to your holy will, for the second death cannot hurt them.

Let us praise and bless the Lord; give him thanks and serve him with great humility.

Neither the first nor the second death could harm Francis. The wound of rejection from his brethren, who moved to a more opulent vision of his charism, was deeply painful. But a second wound lay in store. On the feast of the Assumption, 15 August in 1224, Francis, who had been drafting a new and final version of the Rule in Rome, made his way to La Verna, or Mount Alverna. Here, on the feast of the Exaltation of the Holy Cross, he received another glorious gift from God, the final stamp, the final seal on his life of dedication and trust. Francis received the stigmata; the impression of the wounds of Christ were marked upon his body. Brother Leo, who accompanied him to Mount Alverna takes up the story:

The most blessed Francis, two years before he died, spent Lent at Alverna in honour of the most blessed Virgin Mary, mother of God, and the most blessed archangel Michael. He stayed there from the feast of the Assumption of the holy virgin Mary to the feast of St Michael in September. The hand of the Lord was on him throughout this time. He had the vision and conversation with the Seraphim as well as the impression of the wounds of Christ on his body.

As his final testament to the sisters, Francis would write to Clare:

> I, little Brother Francis, wish to follow the life and poverty of the most high God, our Lord Jesus Christ, and his most holy mother and to persevere in this way to the end. And I beg you, my ladies, and I counsel you to live always in this most holy life of poverty.

These words serve as his own last will and testament. Francis became ill. His eyes, once a gateway to the clear and limpid vision he sought to live by, began to trouble him. His little body let him down. When his death came, he asked to be placed naked on the ground. And so, on 3 October 1226, he died. Stripped, a naked man, the naked man whom God alone could clothe.

The legacy
So what is the legacy and why does this man continue to exert such an influence? There are a variety of reasons. The link with nature is an important one, for Francis, the brother of the

elements and of the animals, offers more than a holistic vision. He is not sentimental or naive about nature because he truly inhabited it. He did not stand on the outside and dream about nature. He began life as a burgher or bourgeois, but then he became a country-dweller, He knew heat and cold and the raw fierceness of the natural world. Nowadays, ecological and green movements have drawn our attention to the need for harmonious living with the planet. Many of their insights, while of considerable importance and backed by scientific study, nevertheless fall short of the vision which Francis entertained. He was not in love with a cosmic force, or with a great inter-planetary dance of life stretching to the edge of the cosmos. He was in love with the divine. God is the Creator and everything is held in relationship within God. That is where true harmony within nature has to be placed. Apart from the Creator, nature can do or be nothing.

This explains why we are mistaken to see Francis as an early environmentalist. He believed that true holiness and freedom come in heaven. He was not concerned to make heaven on earth but to 'rebuild' in the words of the San Damiano experience. He saw the Church which he was to rebuild as a ladder between us and God, God and us; a means of grace; a vehicle for God's love. That is why 'Go, rebuild my church' was a more important command in his world than 'Go, rebuild my planet or my environment' would have been. The love of God led him to experience and to express immense concern for the natural world because, as one God-made creature to another, he identified with it. Nature mirrored something of his own humanity back to him, just as his encounter with the leper had done. The true image of humanity lay in an imperfect, wounded, scarred body, rather than in an apparently perfect one. For a wounded body reminds us of our absolute need for God, just as a wounded planet might do, if we looked at it with the eyes of Francis.

The spirituality of simple acceptance

This sense of the absolute need for God helped Francis embrace poverty with such love and with so little fear. It was central to his spirituality. It restored his humanity to him by returning him to the place of true nakedness, the Garden which God created. This was the Garden of Eden of Genesis chapter 2, in which God was first made known to Adam, the man, and to Eve, as their creator and provider and nurturer. This was also the place where human beings first sinned by denying their humanity and seeking to be gods.

The symmetry of the Incarnation is set up in the Garden of Eden. Only a God who would renounce his divinity and became truly human could redeem us from the deceit of aspiring to be gods ourselves. The Creator becomes our Redeemer. In essence, Francis' choice of poverty is a theological stance of profound spiritual importance rather than an ideological stance or a political one. It asserts this identity of God as our Creator and as our Redeemer. It gives us a religious reality to live by.

So what difference does this make? What wisdom does it offer? First, it offers a vision of creation which puts God at the centre. So in Francis' Canticle, it is God who is blessed and praised, rather than the sun, moon, stars, elements and animals. They exist because God is good, rather than the other way round. Second, Francis offers us a wisdom which knows that human beings, of themselves, are profoundly needy and that our greatest need is for freedom. So, quite uniquely, his theological and spiritual vision enable us to ask what religion is for. Is religion meant to make us nice, for instance? In which case, the next step is for religious people to be nice to each other and to the environment and thereby to build a kinder world. This sounds so simple, and that is part of the snare. For a series of nice ideas about how human beings are to live together fails to take account of original sin. As Francis and his brothers and sisters discovered, the road to heaven is not paved with good intentions. It requires a huge struggle to accommodate people who are different from each other and to enable them to live harmoniously together.

So is religion meant to help us accept that we are not nice? Does it have a utilitarian function, one which offers a vision of a better world both to individuals — as they become more

self-accepting; and to groups or communities —
as they learn to be more tolerant of each other's
crankiness? Take one of the most famous of Old
Testament characters, Jacob, for instance. At the
time of his greatest alienation from God, as he
flees all human encounter because of the terror of
his actions to his brother Esau and the burden of
bitterness in his heart, he dreams of a ladder set
between heaven and earth. That ladder is more
than a powerful image, it is an absolute require-
ment if Jacob is to go to a new place and find
inspiration and glory there. The message is a
simple one. When I acknowledge that I am
deeply flawed, I can read the poet Yeats' words
with a shudder of recognition:

> Now that my ladder's gone
> I must lie down where all the ladders start
> In the foul rag and bone shop of the heart.

There is a ladder for the heart, and Christianity argues that it starts in the 'foul rag and
bone shop of the heart'. As Christians understand it, only that recognition makes true

encounter possible. Anything else excludes the saving work of God and creates a naive theory of human perfectibility. For if we can only bring the nice bits of ourselves to any human encounter, let alone to the encounter we have with God, then what are we to do with our human aggression and competitiveness, with those God-given and deeply primitive techniques we have for human survival? Francis knew about these mechanisms and also about the power of the gospel to set him free from their claims. He knew about self-stripping and the awesome simplicity of a naked encounter with God. The gospel gave him a map for human living because its world was so profoundly God-centred.

The full mystical certainty

That is why he came up with a classic answer to the question, what is religion for? He saw that it is meant to do more than make us nice, or even good. In the name of such a version of religion his contemporaries were going on crusade, resolved to hammer goodness into the infidel. Nor is religion simply meant to help us accept our own sinfulness, though it alone can make us do that. For Francis that would have sat badly alongside his profound sense of the grace and glory of God which are far greater than human wickedness.

Rather he saw that religion, of its essence, brings us into the presence of the transcendent God — and that everything else flows from that. God, our Creator and Redeemer, is also our Sanctifier. This is Trinitarian theology of a high order. It offers a new spiritual vision because our own personal centre gets shifted. We lose our self-absorption when we come into the presence of God and lay aside our anxieties about human living or about our own performance. Francis' mysticism, like the rest of his life, was deeply practical. It did not remove him from human company or human discourse; rather it re-inserted him into them in such a way that his would be an appealing and comforting voice for time and for eternity.

Francis put God first and everything else fell into a new pattern and new design. He was reclothed with splendour because he put on

Christ and was protected and clad by him. God became his all in all. At the end of his life, his body bore the marks of the cross, because he had learnt that simplicity and suffering are normal, for heaven is our true home, where we too will be clothed in glory and where our true radiance lies.

PART THREE

Prayers and Writings

PART THREE

Prayers and Writings

Use these prayers to pray with St Francis of Assisi. Here is his meditation on the Lord's prayer.

Our Father most holy, our Creator, Redeemer, Saviour and Sanctifier.

Who are in heaven. May your kingdom shine in us so that we may know the greatness of your benefits, the breadth of your promises, the height of your majesty and the depth of your judgments.

Your kingdom come. So that you may reign in us by your grace and may bring us into your kingdom, where you are clearly seen, where you are perfectly loved, and known and enjoyed for all eternity.

Your will be done on earth as it is in heaven. We love you with all our heart; we think of you constantly; we desire you with our whole soul; our whole mind is directed towards you. We seek your honour in everything. With all our strength we submit ourselves to you. All our spirits and bodies we submit in obedience to your love. We will love our neighbours as ourselves. We will do our utmost to encourage the whole world to love you. We rejoice with those who rejoice as if their good fortune had been our own. We sympathise with the sad and seek never to offend anyone.

Give us this day our daily bread. Our Lord Jesus Christ, your dear Son, reminds us of the love he has for us and helps us understand it. He makes us venerate all that he has said, done and suffered for us.

And forgive us our trespasses. We are forgiven through your great mercy and because of the passion of your dear Son, our Lord Jesus Christ. We are forgiven through the merits and intercession of the most blessed virgin Mary and of all your elect.

As we forgive them that trespass against us. Grant, O Lord, that even though we do not completely forgive we may nevertheless be completely forgiven. May we truly love our enemies for your sake; may we pray to you devoutly for them and may we give back no-one evil for evil. May we try to be useful to everyone for your sake.

And lead us not into temptation. Lead us not into hidden or open temptations, or sudden or persistent temptations.

But deliver us from evil. Deliver us from past evil, present evil and future evil. Amen.

Francis' vision of harmony and right relationships is the subject of the next extracts from his writings.

We must never seek to dominate others but try to be servants and subject to other people, 'to every human creature for God's sake' (1 Peter 2.13). May the spirit of the Lord rest on everyone who behaves and perseveres to the end in this way. May God dwell in the lives of such people. They will be the sons and daughters of the heavenly Father as they carry out his wishes. They are the husbands, wives, brothers and mothers of our Lord Jesus Christ. We are married to Christ when our soul is sanctified and united to Jesus Christ through the Holy Spirit. We are his brothers and sisters when we do the will of his heavenly Father. We are his mothers when we cherish him in our heart and in our body through pure love and a clear conscience. We do this when we do holy actions for Christ's sake and they are an example to others.

— *Letter to all the Faithful*

Brother Leo, ask for salvation and peace for your Brother Francis! Yes, I speak to you, my son, as a mother, and all that we have said as we travelled along together, I will say again briefly in this letter. I am going to give you some advice about what to do if you want my counsel in the future. Work out the best way to please the Lord God. Follow in his steps and in his poverty. Embrace this way of life with the Lord God's blessing and

in obedience to me. If you seek consolation or
have any other spiritual reason for visiting me,
do come, Leo.

— *Letter to Brother Leo*

*Francis prays in praise of the virtues which he finds in
God and in Mary the mother of Jesus.*

You, Lord and God, are holy, for you alone do
    miracles.
You are strong. You are great. You are the most
    high God.
You are the all-powerful King, the Holy Father,
    the Lord of heaven and earth.
You are the Lord God, three in one, the universal
    good.
You are goodness, universal and supreme, the
    true and living Lord God.
You are kindness and love.
You are wisdom.
You are humility.
You are patience.
You are security.

You are peace.

You are joy and gladness.

You are justice and temperance.

You are all riches which satisfy.

You are beauty.

You are grace.

You are our Protector.

You are our Keeper and Defender.

You are our might.

You are our refreshment.

You are our hope.

You are our confidence.

You are our immense sweetness.

You are our eternal life, our great and adorable Lord, almighty God, merciful Saviour.

— Little Letter to Brother Leo

Holy Virgin Mary, there is no one in the world like you, no woman who has been born in the world like you. You are the daughter and hand-maid of the most high King, the heavenly Father. You are the mother of our most holy Lord Jesus Christ, spouse of the Holy Spirit. Pray for us,

with St Michael the archangel and all the virtues
of heaven and all the saints around your dear and
most holy Son, our Lord and Master.

Antiphon at Compline
from the Easter Triduum Office

Francis lists the fruits of a life of poverty, simplicity
and love.

Greetings, O wisdom, O queen, may the Lord
keep you and your sister simplicity, holy and
pure.

Lady holy poverty, may the Lord keep you and
your most holy sister obedience.

May the Lord keep all of you most holy virtues.

You come from the Lord, your source.

No person in the world can possess a single
virtue unless first dying to self. A person who
possesses one virtue will possess all the
others provided that no harm is done to any
of them. Whoever hurts one of the virtues
offends them all and does not possess any of
them.

67

Each virtue puts vices and sins to confusion.

Holy wisdom confounds Satan and all his devices.

Pure and holy simplicity confounds all worldly wisdom and all human wisdom.

Holy poverty confounds all covetousness, avarice and conformity to this world.

Holy humility confounds pride and all worldly people and all that is in the world.

Holy charity confounds all deep anxieties and the temptations of the flesh and all fear of nature.

Holy obedience confounds all the desires of the body and of the flesh.

Holy obedience keeps the body mortified so that it can obey the Spirit and its brother and sister.

Holy obedience makes a person submissive to all people in the world.

Holy obedience also makes a person submissive to animals, even wild animals, which can do as they wish with him, so long as it is granted to them from above by the Lord.

— *A Greeting to the Virtues*

The work of the Church is a ladder between heaven and earth.

We must also confess all our sins to the priest and receive at his hands the body and blood of our Lord Jesus Christ. The person who does not eat his body and drink his blood cannot enter the kingdom of God.

— Letter to all the Faithful

May the whole world be gripped in fear, may all the people tremble, may the heavens exult when, in the hands of priests, the Christ the Son of the living God descends upon the altar. O amazing splendour, astounding condescension! O sublime humility! The Master of the Universe, God himself and the Son of God, humbles himself so much that he hides himself for our salvation under the feeble appearance of bread. See, brothers, the humility of God and pour out your hearts before him. Humble yourselves so that, in due course, you may be exalted by Christ. Keep nothing of yourselves to yourselves.

— Letter to all the Chapter General

I implore you to ensure that clerics humbly carry out their duties. They should, above all else, venerate the most holy body and blood of our Lord Jesus Christ, his holy name, his written words and the words of consecration. They must treat the chalices, corporals, the ornaments on the altar and everything that is to do with the sacrament as sacred. If the most holy body of the Lord is placed in an obscure place they are to move it reverently to a more prominent place and to administer it with great care. If the names of the Lord and the written words of the Lord are in a dirty area they are to be moved to a clean area.

— *Letter to all the Guardians*

Francis the mystic uses the language of passion and desire, even in times of sickness.

Lord, I pray you, that the burning and bright ardour of your love may detach my soul from all things which are under heaven, so that I may die for love of your love. For you are the One who for love of my love was prepared to die.

— Prayer for Love

Thank you, Lord God, for all the pains with which I am afflicted; I pray you, O my Lord, increase them a hundred times if that is your will. For my great desire is that you spare me neither affliction nor torment. My supreme consolation is in the fulfilment of your holy will.

— Prayer in Time of Sickness

The demands of poverty are absolute.

And if ever, which God forbid, a friar should pick up and appropriate money or a coin, except in the case of necessity for the sick, all the friars regard him as a false brother, as a thief and a robber, as a possessor of goods, until he does penance. Friars shall never collect or arrange any collections for a house or a building and they shall never accompany people who beg in this way. All other offices not contrary to the Rule the friars may undertake with the blessing of God. Nevertheless, friars may beg alms for lepers in case of absolute necessity. But they must fear money greatly. Likewise, all friars must shun searching the world for filthy gain.

— *From the Rule of 1221*

Francis prays in praise of God the Creator, Redeemer and Sanctifier and the whole heavenly host.

Sovereign God Almighty, most high, most holy
most powerful, holy and just Father,
Lord, king of heaven and earth,
We give thanks to you for yourself.
By your will, by your only Son and by your Holy
    Spirit,
you have created spiritual and corporal beings.
You have made us in your image and in your
    likeness
and placed us in paradise,
which through our own fault we have lost.

We thank you that you have created us through
    your Son,

and that because of the holy and true love with
    which you has loved us,

you caused him to be born of the glorious and
    ever-blessed Virgin Mary,

true man and true God.

You willed to redeem us from our captivity

by his cross, his death and his blood.

We thank you because your Son will come

in the glory of his majesty

to drive away into eternal fire the cursed who
    have not repented,

and have not known you,

and to say to those who have known, adored and
    served you with a contrite heart,

'Come, you that are blessed by my Father, inherit
    the kingdom prepared for you from the
    foundation of the world.' (Matthew 25.34)

And because we all, being miserable sinners,

are not worthy to call you by your name,

we humbly pray that our Lord Jesus Christ,

your well-beloved Son in whom you are well
    pleased,

may give you thanks with the Holy Spirit, the
    Sanctifier,
for all your blessings, in a way acceptable to you.
Your Son is all-sufficient,
through whom you have granted us so many
    favours.
Alleluia!

And you, glorious and ever-blessed Mary,
    Mother of God, virgin ever,
blessed Michael, Gabriel and Raphael,
all the choirs of happy spirits,
seraphim, cherubim, thrones, dominions,
    principalities, powers, virtues, angels and
    archangels,
holy John the Baptist, John the Evangelist, Peter
    and Paul,
blessed patriarchs, prophets, saints, innocents,
    apostles, evangelists, disciples, martyrs, con-
    fessors, virgins,
blessed Elijah and Enoch,
and all you holy ones, present, past and to
    come,
we beg you humbly for the love of God

to give thanks to him, the sovereign God, living
   and eternal,
to his dearest Son, our Saviour Jesus Christ,
and to the Holy Spirit, Paraclete,
world without end, Amen. Alleluia!

FURTHER READING

FURTHER READING

Armstrong, Regis J. and Brady, Ignatius C., *Francis and Clare, The Complete Works,* Paulist Press, 1982.

Arnold, Duane and Fry, George, *Francis: A Call to Conversion,* Triangle, 1990.

Backhouse, Halcyon, *The Writings of St Francis of Assisi,* Hodder & Stoughton Christian Classics, 1994.

Celano, Thomas of, *The Lives of S. Francis,* Methuen & Co, 1908.

Chesterton, G. K., *Saint Francis of Assisi,* Hodder & Stoughton, 1923.

Goudge, Elizabeth, *Saint Francis of Assisi,* Hodder and Stoughton, 1961.

Jorgesen, Johannes, *Saint Francis of Assisi,*
Longman, Green & Co., 1912.

Von Matt, Leonard and Hauser, Walter, *Saint
Francis of Assisi,* Longman, Green & Co.,
1956.

Saints for Young Christians

DAVID PREVITALI

Eighty-three fascinating stories relating the lives and experiences of nearly 100 saints are told here in an entertaining, catechetical fashion. Each emphasizes the way in which that particular saint lived the Good News of Jesus in his or her own life. The illustrations enhance the narrative and make it easier for the reader to identify and relate to the saint whose life and works are under discussion. Young people, parents and teachers alike will warm to the solid and yet devotional way in which this work makes the lives of the saints come alive.

Saints Gabriel Possenti, Passionist

GABRIEL CINGOLANI, C.P.

Falling in love is a fundamental event of life. It means not only getting the boy or the girl of one's dreams, but above all finding a reason for living life passionately. Francis Possenti of Assisi, who became Gabriel of Our Lady of Sorrows as a Passionist, fell in love with a girl, as was normal for an 18-year-old boy. But when he realized that there was also another way to fulfill himself in an overflowing of love: by spending his life for God and others. He gave himself so completely that at 24, his life had been used up. This is his story.

Thérèse of Lisieux and
Marie of the Trinity

PIERRE DESCOUVEMONT

Marie-Louis Castel was 20 years old when she entered the Carmel of Lisieux in 1894 and became the novice of St. Thérèse of the Child Jesus. For the next 50 years she put into practice in her daily life the "little way" taught to her by her saintly novice mistress. Suffering terribly from a painful facial ulcer in the final years of her life, she remained always faithful to "the spirituality of the smile." Her favorite saying which she had learned from St. Thérèse and which she was known often to repeat was, "No! Life is not sad!" It's an attitude and outlook on life that is found on every page of this inspiring work.